S. NOYES
GRATEFULLY
POSSESSED!

Coming to Terms

Coming to Terms

POEMS BY

Josephine Miles

University of Illinois Press

Urbana   Chicago   London

Library of Congress Cataloging in Publication Data

Miles, Josephine, 1911–
Coming to terms.

I. Title.
PS3525.I4835C6   811'.5'2   79–18235
ISBN 0–252–00767–0
ISBN 0–252–00768–9 pbk.

Acknowledgment is made to the publications in which
some of these poems have appeared: *Ascent, Beloit
Poetry Journal, California Quarterly, Gramercy Review,
Hawaii Review, Hyperion, Mill Mountain Review, New
England Review, The New Yorker, Plainsong, Poetry Now,
The San Jose Quarterly, UCSD, Woman Poet, Yank.*

Contents

Trip

We started from a station in the city,
Rough night, wind blowing rain slantwise
On the train windows.
Outside was the elegance of the station,
Hothouse roses in the areas
Of people saying goodbye,
Good luck.
We were the ones going
Into a tunnel of dark
Crying those going-away blues, going-away blues
In our long black woolen stockings and button shoes.
Hail, hail the gang's all here
Sang my father to the mahogany walls.
We were not listening and would not sing
What do we care. But we heard him.
The train pulled out of the station into Halloween,
The train pulled into November and the passengers between
Pumpkin and pumpkin gave us some good scares
To wile away the Halloween blues.
Three days and nights in the vestibules
Between cars, roaring and clashing at the heavy doors,
Closer to home than the outside scenes.
Then a little
Five minute flash of home
El Paso is The Pass, my mother said
But it was rather
A burning deck of people in sombreros
Sitting against the sun. Rejoicing.
Now we could see orange trees, smell orange, that was a
        wonder,
And came through that garden to a narrow track
Of train on sand between mountains

Splitting against their ledges,
Nearly empty
The coaches, ledges, rocking along, seeking
Places to stop, with yellow stations
Under pepperwood, under water tank, under signal
Under sky
Nearly empty but our smoke blew in it.
All the baggage is gathered together, we stand
At the last vestibule, we are saying goodbye,
Good luck.
We pile down, look at the little
Boards of the station, turn away
Back to our black coaches, all of us in a row
In our black woolen stockings in the burning sun
To watch them leave us, pull away one by one
With a great grinding.
And they are gone.
And I see, what do we see, all of us,
Stretching my gasping eyes without air or kindness,
Sandy ranges of an infinite distance
Under a white hot sky under
Infinite distance
Beyond a plain, a sea, a life of sand
Of infinite distance
No place to end. A breadth
Hurtful to any small heart
A scope which beached our débris on its shore
Abandoned, lost from a tide of life.
Extended
Not toward us but away,
But we went to it.

Thirsty we drank its infinite sources
Eyes brimmed with its tears.
A hotelkeeper in pith hat and jodhpurs
Drove our baggage into the Springs, in oasis,
But we had gone farther away.

4

Before

Earlier, what I remember: a small
Flame of arthritis in the midst of fields
In the Euclidean Sunday mustard fields
And the mud fields of the potted palm,
In Jackie's airy room,
And at the fire station
All the brass
And all of us
Feeding the gulls.
A fresh salt breeze and foam
Around a plaster leg.

Away from the chloroform intern, joy
Of the long journey when I ran
Free of the plaster, and got back
Down those long hills, spent out.
Where had I been, oh tell me.
And where
Under those vast sunny
Apricot trees in the front yard?
Go tell Aunt Rhodie the old gray goose is dead.

Blocks

Earlier, many chloroformed halls went through,
White sheets lay on,
Masks breathed into,
Sotto voices calibrated.
They were all brick walls
Rising from root level below ground
To beyond eyesight
Standing across some sun.
Scotched by their presence,
Went with Mme. Montessori home again.

Motive

A window in the shadowed room where I lay
Opened on a dark brick wall
And high beyond, the sooty block
Of buildings stood in rain.

Heat in bones under blankets burned
With aspirin. Keeping me warm,
What else? Grandfather shrugged.
Stepgrandmother reheated the hot milk.

Later she brought also a small box
Which turned out to be filled with six small bottles
Of perfumes, assorted, six colors,
Oho! There is something to life!

Doll

Though the willows bent down to shelter us where we played
House in the sandy acres, though our dolls,
Especially Lillian, weathered all the action,
I kept getting so much earlier home to rest
That medical consultation led to cast
From head to toe. It was a surprise for my parents
And so for me also, and I railed
Flat out in the back seat on the long trip home
In which three tires blew on our trusty Mitchell.
Home, in a slight roughhouse of my brothers,
It turned out Lillian had been knocked to the floor and
        broken
Across the face. Good, said my mother
In her John Deweyan constructive way,
Now you and Lillian can be mended together.
We made a special trip to the doll hospital
To pick her up. But, they can't fix her after all, my father
        said,
You'll just have to tend her with her broken cheek.
I was very willing. We opened the box, and she lay
In shards mixed among tissue paper. Only her eyes
Set loose on a metal stick so they would open
And close, opened and closed, and I grew seasick.

A friend of the family sent me a kewpie doll.
Later Miss Babcox the sitter
After many repetitious card games,
Said, we must talk about bad things.
Let me tell you
Some of the bad things I have known in my life.
She did not ask me mine, I could not have told her.
Among the bad things in my life, she said,
Have been many good people, good but without troubles;
Her various stories tended
To end with transmigrations of one sort or another,
Dishonest riches to honest poverty; kings and queens
To indians over an adequate space of time.
Take this cat, coming along here, she said,
A glossy black cat whom she fed her wages in salmon,
He is a wise one, about to become a person.
Come to think of it, possibly Lillian
Is about to become a cat.
She will have different eyes then, I said.
Obviously. Slanted, and what is more,
Able to see in the dark.

Parent

Letting down the isinglass curtains
Between the wet rain and the back seat
Where new plaster flattened me, my father said,
Wait here. I will get you the sherbet
Of your eight-year-old dreams.
There were no drive-ins then.
The rain roared. Don't go away,
I said to him? He said to me.

Album

This is a hard life you are living
While you are young,
My father said,
As I scratched my casted knees with a paper knife.
By laws of compensation
Your old age should be grand.

Not grand, but of a terrible
Compensation, to perceive
Past the energy of survival
In its sadness
The hard life of the young.

Mark

Irritated by the favoritism of Jehovah
Fatherhood of God,
I thought Cain
Into the wilderness. Southern Pacific
Set up in the mesquite trees
Yellow station boards
To split and wither in the shattering heat,
And there I saw
Necessity. Blessed necessity.
Blessed ground, blessed shade
Blessed telegraph, cactus
Necessity.
To which the vulnerable parent
Nodded and smiled.

Violets

Flat markets in the flat rain,
Wet wool of being
Yet damper to receive in its sharpless squares
Hurtful if need be.
Whereas from my mother violets come to the wet wool,
From accidental deep bins of produce
And bespeak
Sources beyond price, beyond hesitation.

Oceans at Eighteen
1929–1932

NAME

Father, father, says the sea's edge,
Crumpling under my window.

That is a word I have not said;
It lies in my head
But I speak it not.
The sea teaches me
To remember quietly
What my tongue has forgot.
Father is a word my tongue once said;
Now it knows other names instead.

Father, father, remembers the sea,
Quietly under my window.

DIALOGUE

You're like a still pool in the rocks, he told her,
You hear the thudding of a surf far off.
You feel the surging of the sea's mountains
Up and down the long green mountain pathways
Only as a bright and silver ripple
Of a fish swimming somewhere. Wake up, he cried,
And move with the fierce motion of the sea.
She shifted her feet under her, as a pool does, softly.
See this red pebble?—I love red ones, she said.

MORNING IN BRANCHES

Year upon year of sunlight lying here,
Decades of gold upon a length of bark;
Archaic speech of leaves that spin their shadows
To fitful flecks of dark:

This time will end with death of shade at noon
As crescent light began it, long ago.
This branch and I will be a morning older—
Year upon year of sunlight older than you know.

SPEED LIMIT

There is a heap of sky out tonight, brother,
There is a heap of air round and about.
Speed on this road, turn off on another,
And we'll go out.

Out into the wide sky,
Suddenly.

Keep two wheels down on the street here, brother,
Curves have a way of riding on wind tonight.
Hill on one side, air on every other,
We'll stick tight.

Tight to the small ground moving steadily
In so much sky!

INVASION

With doors banging in the bright morning
We turn upon wind.
And the sound of cars on tracks, of sparrows, of speech
Is excessively thinned.
Under the dining room table sits the wind.

Clocks in towers whisper the hours
Galley-west.
But the echoes of bells are fleetly shredded and swept
Under the dining room table with the rest
Of the dust in the wind's nest.

The shaken doors beat sunlight on the floors.
Seas leap ahead.
And leaves, feet, faint shouting, and wings
Roughly are sped
Over an earth now doubly inhabited.

Salute

Riding along the desert highway in any old car
I would dreamily nod
To trees standing and waving along the way.
I would graciously bow, recognize
Their beauty of attention.

Ruefully I may think back to that world
Of friendly accord, riding now
In golden fields scattered with lone oak trees,
Now I may know
It was the realm of the trees I rode in, not of mine.

Rest

Right at the freeway where the sounds
Drift up the canyon, the Sunday rush
Rush begins early, lines of cars
Close on each other, dash to dash, follow

Across the gap and in the swale resound
The rush and rush, resources heavily
Lent in green fields and going on,
A measure of the day.

But then some closure sends a delicate drift
Of sounds like pottery splintered, lightly enough
Leading off a siren long, to be silenced
As Sunday finally lends its shattered rest.

Text

How get water, have, keep it
These are the questions of the wild and human.
Continents rise as the shores rise, granite
And this hard pale rock of quartz and feldspar,

As at the railroad bridge near the city pond, will
Force the water up
Or at the steep and barren sides in downpour
Will let it go.

Study

At midnight dropping the beautiful
White net dress, I could not think
To be rid of it in sleep, to prepare
A flying spirit for a Saturday test.
There went joy, celebration, and there came
Heavy suppression to a lofty norm.

Saturday sulk and blur, everyone went
To the beach, I to a Hall under vines.
The sun shone in, the topic was either,
To my reckoning, Progress of Science,
Or Music in the Home. A sum of words.
There I prayed to friends, Franklyn, Frances, Dorothy,
        Roberta, as once to Welda,
Don't write on Murk in the Home! They did though.

My brothers were painting trim when I got to the cabin,
And said to our father, it is the wrong shade,
But my light heart jolted me out from that message,
To pause on the one I'd got in the afternoon light
Carved in the archway over that lively moss,
"Education is learning to use the tools
Which the race has found indispensable."

I thought, Good for Education, modest, and steadily
Learning its way. Out of that shabby gentle world of Melrose
Out toward the sea and the ranges
Of Greek and geology. Learning the tools.

Teacher

How did you come to be a teacher?
I went to work
In the Huntington Library in San Marino,
The many treasures unopened and uncut
Gave me pause.
Summer as it was, hot as it was, the best part of the day
Was a Chapman's ice cream cone with Jim Worthen,
Before Hollywood Bowl or Pasadena Playhouse,
To learn to write plays.
One practicing day in the heavy Fresno sunlight,
One practicing year in Berkeley fog,
Lehman, Caldwell, Lyon, Dennes,
The steady hearts of scholars made me be.

How did I come to be a teacher.
Another way.
On the street where I lived, two boys were going to college,
One to Cal Tech and one to Business School
—This is a little simpler than it was—
And both were in terrible struggles over learning
Especially by thought, like reason and consequence,
So I could help them.
That is pretty much of a joy
For fifteen to help nineteen and twenty-three
To engineer arguments, try Shakespeare, evaluate
Albers Mills for Dun and Bradstreet.
So that's how.

Readers

Jeff thinks
This is an angry text.
The professor asks how does he know
Is he right? Will he profess?
Later today I will ask
Is it an angry text? Does he know my mind?
Over this famous text hovers a shadow.
Slowly it moves, the while in the temperate air
Flails Jeff's hand and flails mine,
I am angrier than he.
Sometimes with strength of resistance the teacher
Holds back the visible hands,
There is scarcely time for the lot,
And says listen and wait.
Protecting the text, protecting, then does he know
Jeff's anger and mine?

Disarmed

Here an establishment, its sunny rooms,
Noon offices and beings, vast competitive
Orders, clashes of temper,
Hope forward, elegant energy
Unfolded and disarmed me,
Turned to a love so swift it went
In and beyond that world like a free runner and found
Bodies of love out of belief.
Love of demeanor, love of that face and form
Just as it moved, seldom as I saw it
Put back together in my asking frame
A fortune of demeanor shapely and true.

Slack

As slack mouth spills information,
Lip loosely widened slurs it
Hand takes it on, curves and holds,
Wrist weighs, lays it along,
Gives it to me,
I accept, and thank the hand,
Though it's the slack says I'm welcome.

Sleeve

This was a dark year for Spiro Agnew;
It was a dark year for me too.
I like fathers and brothers, I like to grow
Toward the height, following it, a shoulder of sun.

I lean on this shoulder and it bears me up
Wide, well-suited, strong and square,
It holds my need, all I need
Rests there,

Substance of trust;
But this year touch my sleeve; my sleeve rends
In the dark, in the hidden dust,
To moth and rust.

Fanatic

Conference rolls on, chairs are hard,
Members on the flag-decked platform
Heard and unheard.

In the wings, doors watched by students,
Flutters of white, now and then, become
As out of vaults,

Multitudes of white-robed figures, arms lifted,
Flowing smoothly over auditorium seats
And consuming them.

Here and there, little clusters of listeners
Sit tight. I sit tight and hear
Phagocytes.

Clusters disappear, the silent fanatic
Coverage
Pure as fine linen.

Payment

The time sticks, the crazy anaesthetic
Bloodless brain and open throat,
Wild weak angry coming home,
The ambulance orderly listing at each intersection
Fatal accidents he had seen there,
What parts severed, what held by a thread.
Under the sycamores, past my mother cracked by the gate,
My stretcher carried all the falling leaves,
Until I found my checkbook under me
And wrote the slipshod check.
Weak, wild, a saccharine
Taste in every food, and saccharine
In every voice I asked help of.
Slowly his help, the sharp egotist's,
Slowly avoiding the favors of his colleagues,
Slowly turns to pillow, footsole, diet,
These smaller makeshifts in their saltier tones.
My barbed-wire heart
I turn on when I turn
Keeps count the compromises of his role, deepening
As skill concedes to sense.

Morning

A picture window opening to the west
Is curtained in the morning; from the outside
It's a closed room. From the inside,
Gloom. The sun collaborates,
West gray in shade.
Now I must ask you whether a leaf of sun
Will gradually cast its tentative light within
Or whether you will proceed across the floor
Pull back the drapes and look into the day
As if you would renew it? From the outside
A scene of limitless shape, a chandelier
Bathed in reflection, each corner
Each morning
As if the furnished action had no fear
To act again.

Breakfast

Robert keeps in his parlor
A beautifully wrought casket
With a lady in it
Of Chinese descent, and a bouquet of orchids.

In his backyard he grows
Plots of chard,
And plucks it
Fresh as desire for dinner and breakfast.

Much comment
On the Swiss chard its freshness, savor,
Sweetness, suitability, seems to prevent
Any comment on the orchid bouquet.

Luncheon

Jack Lyman came down from St. Helena for luncheon.
A warm day
In the vineyard valley, misty in Berkeley.
Rosalie Brown, *The Grasshopper's Man,* came, and Leonard
    Nathan,
Who Is Tolstoi, and Carol his wife.
Ask him
Were the eucalyptus groves in Berkeley like this then
When the Greek dancers danced in groves
As if fog, in chiffon? Where was the red wine
Inkiest in the city? How
Did Witter Bynner win those champions
From brief vignettes of song?

Later in the backyard
Leonard and I read the Rhymer's Club
To try to hear what they heard, but that wasn't it—
Those were ballads, in London, this may be George Sterling,
Evanescent?
At Arts and Crafts,
Kroeber, Cody's, Moe's, John's Soup Kitchen,
Far from the traffic of the Greek Theater,
They are crying or they are stammering
Creeley's halt lines.

So we ask Lyman at lunch,
As we would Hildegarde Flanner, Genevieve Taggard,
What did you hear then? Tell us how we can hear.
    Elusively, a sense of things unheard
    Awakes, and is forgotten as it dies.
    The afternoon is great with peace. Then cries
    Far off, and once, a bird.
From *Sails and Mirage and Other Poems,*
By George Sterling.

Luncheon 2

We met for luncheon to exchange views,
Soviet authors and ours, two Armenians
And a writer of children's stories,
Beef stew and jello, but no shared language
So we say, Pasternak? No, no, their anger.
Gogol? More kindly, shake hands.
Sroyán? Aha! you happy people,
He walks among the pomegranate rows.

Dear friends, we exchange cards,
Minor titles and their authorship.
How much we know each other, drink our tea.
Then comes the tardy interpreter, checks all round
In Russian, and then asks us,
Why did you drop the bomb on Hiroshima?

Noon

Noon students slid onto the unfolded chairs
In the open square where Aldous Huxley stood.
He said, you will be told by those supposed
Wiser, that reason and intuition

Work together, support each other.
But that is false.
Reason is the great saboteur.
Do not believe otherwise.

Two o'clock class: What do I believe?
I believe otherwise.

Goodbye

Did I make you angry, said Jim the Professor
To Daphne the four-year-old child.
She said nothing.

Please accept my regrets,
Said Jim the Professor
To Daphne. She said nothing.

I've got to go off to class now, said Jim
Astride his bike. Won't you say goodbye?
She said nothing.

Off down the road he went in a flurry of shirttails
Blurring into the wind, and rounding the corner
Out of sight. Goodbye, said Daphne.

Poetry, Berkeley

When Seamus Heaney was staying a year in Berkeley
Lyman Andrews came back from England in summer,
And paid him a visit.
They had a drink together and chatted,
While Seamus's five-year-old Michael played with his cars.
Did you know my daddy before? Michael inquired.
No, this is the first time we've met, smiled Lyman.
Then how did you know to come to the house?

Officers

Mr. Hansen, the cop at the campus gate,
Put me through college.
While the dean of women
Advised against it, too complicated, the cop said
You get enrolled some way, and I'll let you in.
Every morning, four years. On commencement day
I showed him my diploma.

Later when radio news announced Clark Kerr
President, my first rejoicing
Was with Mr. Taylor
At the campus gate. He shook hands
Joyfully, as I went in to a Marianne Moore reading.
And we exchanged over many years
Varying views of the weather.

Then on a dark night a giant officer came up to the car
When we were going to a senate meeting, strikebound by
        pickets,
And smashed his billy club down on the elbow of my student
        driver.
Where do you think you are going? I suddenly saw I knew
        him.
It's you, Mr. Graham, I mean it's us, going to the meeting. He
        walked away
Turning short and small, which he was, a compact man
Of great neatness.

Later when I taught in the basement corridor,
The fuzz came through,
Running, loosing tear gas bombs in the corridor
To rise and choke in offices and classrooms,

Too late for escape. Their gas masks distorted their
      appearance
But they were Mr. O'Neill and Mr. Swenson.

Since then, I have not met an officer
That I can call by name.

Memorial Day

After noon, in the plaza, cries, shrill yells, running and
    breaking,
Students look desperately
Out of the open windows. We have to be there.
A rifle waves in the window,
Tear gas gusts in, no one to help
In the furtherance of this class in Milton's epics.
Well let's meet tomorrow at my house.
OK, we'll bring the wholegrain wheat germ raisin bread.
Up in the office floors, out in the square,
Gas of a new kind in experimentation.
I choke and cry the tears they call for.
    So I say, and now we are munching
Crunchies in the front yard,
And finishing the patristic part of Book VII,
Papers are due after the weekend,
Please go home and work there,
And tell your parents the story of these weeks.
Even if they believe in the war you're protesting,
They will believe you too. Tell them
The sorts of pressures, absences of aid,
Losses of understanding you are working under.
They say they've already tried: I get my dad on the phone
And he says You can't tell me.
Give me Mom, and my Mom says
You can't tell me. Stay out of trouble.
The army helicopter
In its regular rounds of surveillance, drops down low—
Our twenty figures in a courtyard may mean trouble.
Couldn't we pick these flowers to throw at them?
All these camellias overgrown and wasting?

Institutions

At term end the institution slackens
And I have done poorly, not what I hoped.
So my thought is seized by other institutions
More terrible, where I would do less well.
Hospital, asylum, prison, prison camp,
And I fall into a reverie of dismay:
Failure to aid survival, failure to foster,
Failure to understand how the oppressions start.
End of term, cease of a striving heart.

Or term end and I have done well in it
Much that I hoped, much that I tried,
And I am caught from these visions into a stupor
Of all the more I have left untried.
Hospital, asylum, prison, tiger cage
Beyond my thought like a rift of cloud.
Shelter me from unending need, term end,
Begin a new demand.

Figure

A poem I keep forgetting to write
Is about the stars
How I see them in their order
Even without the *chair* and *bear* and the *sisters,*
In their astronomic presence of great space,
And how beyond and behind my eyes they are moving
Exploding to spirals under extremest pressure.
Having not mathematics, my head
Bursts with anguish of not understanding.

The poem I forget to write is bursting fragments
Of a tortured victim, far from me
In his galaxy of minds bent upon him,
In the oblivion of his headline status
Crumpled and exploding as incomparable
As a star, yet present in its light.
I forget to write.

Barricade

Work hard and fail
Stop right at the wall
Look around at the no-saying mouths, turn away,
What can you say? Walk away.

Pick up a new track, few there
Clear it away,
Press on in the clear air
And the breath
Of the others, and fail.

Stop in your track
At the sudden superfluous crowd saying stop,
Saying no. Pick up a trail
Dense as a jungle and friendly with friends, and go on
In a different direction
To rising and setting of sun
And be stopped, and say fail.

Shall you return?
By the barrows of age shall you move
Back on those tracks where the walls were?
Where are they now?
The bafflement comes to the resting and tiresome foot
Of a thousand of roads
All open, all asking traverse.

Metamorphosis

At Johns Manville a miscalculation
Sent more asbestos fibres into the assembly-line air
Than would kill a cat. Tough Texans
Long laughed as they breathed.
After the first deaths, some investigations
By the Company, the Medical Profession, and the US Bureau
    of Health
Came up with findings,
That is, with true facts,
That is with data, that is with knowledge.

And knowledge is power. The data
Were stacked on a high shelf and grew dusty
With asbestos dust.
Finally a young doctor, a student
Of mine, and I wish he were,
Got the stacks off the shelf.
Now the plant has been razed
And the coughers scattered to their various deaths.

Giant Texans breathing through calcium
Of too much recommended, it was said, milk,
Stir into the altitudes of the A M A
Of H E W, Johns Manville,
Some of your rough laughter, that they wake
You to their learning, making you put on
Their knowledge with their power.

Bureau

Is this the University?
I'm calling about a letter of recommendation I want to
    withdraw.
What's the extension, 4101?
This is the Library.
Then how will I find the number of the Bureau
Of Employment, maybe it's Placement?
I'll give you the Director.
I merely want to withdraw and reword a letter.
This is Mr. McShaw, the Director. Yes, here is your item,
Professor, this is an excellent letter,
It must not be withdrawn.
Read Fowler, Strunk and White, any of the authorities
You will see how well you have done here.
Pardon my exercise of authority,
But I cannot allow a good letter to be withdrawn.
Is this the University?
I am calling about bureaus; their hearts and minds.

Bureau 2

Skunks fight under the house and keep us
Wakeful, they are down from the hills in the drought.
Lots of colloquial remedies, mothballs, tomato juice
Leave them unmoved. Call the S P C A.
Call the Bureau of Health, call the P G & E where they rest
Past the meter box, call the Animal Shelter,
Call commercial exterminators; all reply
With a sigh, and a different number to call
Next month or next year when they're not so busy.
Asking around, getting the number finally
Number of the chief health officer of the county,
Mr. Simms. His secretary answers,
What makes you think Mr. Simms will speak to you?
What makes you think Mr. Simms is interested in skunks?
Mr. Simms is animal health officer of this whole county
And his chief interest is wolves.

Moving In

The telephone-installer was interested
In the students helping me.
He said he had a father of 93, plus a mother 77
And his wife kept running her heart out.
Students could help, what a good idea! Let me know
If at any time this telephone needs adjusting.

As he left, the upstairs apartment entered
With some slices of chocolate angel food cake
To make herself acquainted.
She was a retired librarian and it turned out
The one librarian I knew in the town I came from
Was an old friend of hers, they both came
From South Dakota mining country.

The telephone-installer returned to ask
If students were dependable? They can be.
Even more than a good chocolate cake, even more
Than a good telephone.
This could mean a new life for my wife and me, he said,
I think I'll bring you a longer cord for that phone.
Don't let this last piece of cake go begging, begged the
        upstairs apartment.

Concert

I was sitting behind a somewhat neat old person
In creamlined beige matching coat and hat
Neat but that the hat crown
Tilted at a curious angle left to right.
As I deliberated, she turned her head impatiently
As at a draft of air,
And pulled the hat from off a mane of hair,
Of wild white hair.

Concert 2

One brings her cane
To hook on to her purse, which holds a shoe
And a ladle, and at intermission
Fights her way to the refreshments.

I see her with such eyes I feel like a macho
Cyclist harrassing a small town
To bully the scattering citizens
And to set fires in doorways.

Fund Raising

When Genét came with the Panthers
To raise defense funds,
The Treuhafts stood him on a ladder before their old
    clinker-brick fireplace.
The bulky man,
Bursting in French English,
His clenched fist swayed the ladder, his wrath
Leaned into the social press.
He smiled at Masao, and spat also,
From his compact smooth density of resources.
Hilliard yelled, and others yelled
Until finally someone picked up a bottle
And threw it at someone.
It struck Michael McClure's young daughter
Where she sat on the hearth
And she sobbed, sobbed. Michael, schooled as a flame,
Leaped to the ladder and cried in a whisper
Victims! Always we have to have victims.
Down the steps of the porch, into cars,
Nobody there.

Why We Are Late

A red light is stuck
At the corner of LeConte and Euclid.
Numbers of people are going in and out of the 7 Palms
     Market,
Some sitting with beer at La Vals,
Lots lugging bags to the Laundromat—Open—
A couple thumbing rides up the hill, fog curling in over the
     newsracks,
Low pressures.

You can tell it is about five or six o'clock
And we are coming home from a meeting not bad, not good,
Just coming along, and stop at the red light.
Time stands there, we in the midst of it,
The numberless years of our lives.
A late green light later
May let us get home.

Evening News

You know how the newsboy bikes through the stubblefield,
On the faint rough path between wild vines,
Into the condominium complex, the one hundreds
Then the two hundreds,
Hurling *Enterprises* as he rides?
Why does he suddenly ride in the opposite direction?
Why do the galaxies shift in the opposite direction?

At the Counter

Give me a half sack of buttered popcorn, sweetie.
Would you like to hear some good news?
I'm a biochemist you know, even look like a biochemist they
    tell me,
Despite my rugged frame.
And today I discovered the cure for diabetes!
You may well exclaim.

You know what the cure is? an herb. It grows high
In the mountains of Mexico.
And my doctor tells me that my big chest cavity
Enlarged from singing opera will allow
My living as high as sixteen thousand feet
To cultivate the herb. What is its name?
I bet you'd like to know!

Supper

They came through the late summer light
Dr. Feldenkrais and his assistants,
Through the tall doors,
To hear Bea read her Crazy Jane for them,
We were just finishing coffee, and they explained
They were so prompt after their long day
Because they had eaten nothing. Helen said,
I can give you roast beef, french bread, salad, lasagna,
Before Bea reads.

Feldenkrais beamed, sat at the long table, began telling
About the brain. Did we know Gurdjieff?
Platters and platters, so eat and eat,
Platelets of memory around the ribs
Rattle the brain.
That's just what I'm teaching, said Helen.
See here on page ten of this book I teach from.
Remarkable, pondered the master; your name is Helen?
Yes, more lasagna.

Talk in the darkening room of the house of Jim's mother,
As it was called, where we had celebrated
Swinging feet, eating brownies,
Birthdays at the long table.
Have a brownie, Dr. Feldenkrais.
Bea's Crazy Jane, words
For music perhaps.

Trade Center

When Leopold Senghor came to America
To negotiate with the President about imports
Such as lobster tails, he was asked at the White House
      luncheon
Whether he would go to Disneyland
As Khrushchev had not.
No, but, he said,
I will go to meet the boys of Hunter's Point
And the poets of San Francisco.
Seven o'clock, the wide windows of the Trade Center
Opened east over the bay,
To the low hills of Berkeley; lights and silver gleamed.
Senghor with his four short round ambassadors
Entered in French.
Where I sat listening in French, questioning in English
About alexandrines, the kindly interpreter
Wafted himself away from that metric region
Of half-understanding. At dinner,
The Liberian ambassador, expert in American,
Put us into hilarity over the common procedures
Of Liberian diplomacy; would we not laugh we would cry,
How in his mint-julep stories we were children.
Then with a gasp
Poet and ambassadors pushed back their chairs,
Stood and bowed low
Out past the black windows to where in the east
Full over the hills into the blackest of summer skies, ascended
Their own moon.

Pearl

Inside the plane we went straight
Off the round earth into the round air,
Rounder, as if into a pearl,
A pearl's center, rounder, walls of pearl
Awash, luminous in the swim of pearl.

On our raft, luggage, small glasses, unexpandable
Into existences of milk and pearl,
Raft from Peoria, pitching in the sea
Of Galatea, floating
A few words of pidgin into pearl.

Delay

Well, ladies and gentlemen, the tinned voice of the pilot said,
We seem to be having trouble with the landing gear
Which is why you hear this loud shaking sound.
We are therefore returning to home port, hope to land
Without incident, will keep you informed.
The stewardesses worked on equipment in their booth.
Then many of the ladies and gentlemen
Moved from where they sat in holiday or business absorption
Over next to some child and engaged
In a great deal of peaceful conversation—
Reminiscences of their own, sighs, questions of the children,
Till the gear
Jolted itself into landing, and the pilot
Came on again, to regret the inconvenience.

Travelers

The little girl was traveling unattached, as they say,
Closed into the window-seat by a heavy
Businessman working on papers out of his briefcase.
From across the aisle another kept noticing
What help she needed, her travel-case latched,
Her doll righted, coloring-book straightened out,
And he kept leaning over across to assist her.
After a while the heavyset man put away his papers,
Took out a small gameboard from his briefcase, and
        suggested,
How about a game of three-way parcheesi?

Island

On the island each figure
Moves to become its island,
Down to the shore, enters
The surrounding sea.
Is surrounded
By the waves of its waters
Crowding its beaches.

A fringe of palms, or pines maybe,
Touch
Some outlying strand,
The center tingles
Toward opposite reaches.
Each figure
Wades fully into the waters of his island, saying
I am land.

Lone

Braking down a stretch of coast highway,
Enough sand shoulder for the VW to pull toward
When it starts dragging its rear end like a dog,
Back, how many miles of breakers?
Ahead, a promontory bend in the road.
No one passes, and the stillness extends.
Scrape the split axle around the point,
And see what's there,
Some sort of joint beyond the marine zero?
Dragtail the pavement half mile, mile, and turn
And there appear a leaning porch and pump,
Three signs: *Gas, Nehi, Wrecking Crew.*
They stand by the pump, the bottles in their hands.

Intensives

Loving intensives of Intensive Care
Bear down on your given name,
Margaret, attend, attend now
Margaret, they call you to live intensely
At the moment of your medication.

What if for a while they call you Frances?
Enjoy this intensive
Error, it frees you,
You can float in Frances,
Sip Frances liquids.

What I wait for is the intensive moment
When you flip, turn over, look around.
Well, hello, Dolly, back where
Hello, Dolly,
Where you belong.

Sorrow

A tall stature of
Grave sorrow
Is what I embrace, its tenderness
Doesn't bend to me.
Straight

Sorrow descended
From cries in trees
Stands upright
Stiff at its waist
Where I reach,

Tells me but does not
Tell me.
Rather withholds
More than I can
More than man can.

Weed

As weed swells to its joint
    brittles its root
    slants at a bent
    angle and
    cracks in the sun, one
can believe
that many years have gone
since the green sprout sprang,
each flick of green
    momentous as a time
    to chew the remnant stem.

Paper

This soft paper
Asks a soft answer,
Asks to think of mohair
Nimble
Silky
Poised, eyes lidded
In a soft light.
And the wire-lines of the paper
Carry its question
Literally
From word to word.

Manifold

In the cabinet of analysis
Seeds group themselves by seed,
Catalogues invest a native cyclamen
Which knows no bond.

Curves to the manifold seem to subscribe
In parallel measure,
And in the flour bin the soy
Scatters to flour.

Lets off the hook a rigid
Marking of rights and signs
For the sake of savor,
Geometries of change.

Brim

Less of time than the world allows
A repeated task, sinews not taking
Supposed messages, where will we be
Under the reign of senex? I absolve him
Of many miseries.

Curry another time, other worldly,
But here at home
Turn to skies in their wheeling
A simple crowded passage across the brim.

Nadirs

There were the clerks of the zenith and the figures,
There were winter-type clouds over the winter
There were summer-type clouds over the summer figures
And to speak to each there was a way, the same.
I went up to the clerk of the nadir and said see me
In noctions of one kind or another
Under a winter sun, and see safely to the zenith
How I welter under a blooming moon.
All is mine, but I like it
By each gesture toward the other or one.
So besit, said the clerks of the nadir
And the zenith as they turned to their own
Accounting of afternoon—
They were busy. How busy were they?
They required waiting in line
For the sun to go down over the eastern figures
And the moon to arise over the western figures
Moving from plane to plane.

Easter

Cars drove in at angles
All around the flat adobe mission
Coming for Mass.
White carnations
Were stuck before each saint of the desert
And tied with lavender ribbons.
A bucket held the water to be blessed;
A jug, the wine;
And the microphone kept tangling with tall candles
Before the lectern, before the altar.

Wiry twisted field workers came,
And polished uniforms from the air base;
And a group of sisters from the seminary
Made the responses sing in experienced voices,
Two hundred, because of the resurrection.
They had to push away the plywood back of the altar
And screen doors from the sides to take the numbers,
And the choir crowded in to make room.

Beside me sat three little dark girls
In yellow print dresses and crocheted stoles,
And before me their father, his heavy shoulders
Sloped over the slant of an easy hip,
His drawled notes to his wife with her beehive hairdo
Getting from her many worried frowns, sometimes a
        luminous smile;
They followed their missalettes from page 26
To page 31, and page 56
And they brought him to the tomb.

Hello, folks, glad to have you with us
On this auspicious occasion when he is risen.
Some of you will want to take the blessed wine and the
        blessed wafer
And receive communion. And this evening mass will count
As a Sunday mass also. God be with you.
The tides that rose

In seas and trees
In the barometers of sealed test tubes
Rose with this moon over the desert
And I could see how the candles
Survived the entanglements of the microphones.
Everything there, in fact, rose from its tomb
And went along the road to Emmaus.

Makers

I would tell a tally of poets
With their black interests.
When they can eat, they pay
Out of their nourishment they produce
Duck eggs, reindeer meat, seldom herbivorous.
Printers make their hearts go,
Run the links of their nucleic acids.
Small interest says our investor,
Small but compounded.

A letter out of the grain-filled San Joaquin Valley
Came to me whirlwind.
Change everything, be somebody else
Commit other and less trivial sins,
That was my Brother Antoninus. But the great sins
Which the world at war called him to commit
He did not commit. He craved against his sainthood.

Change also said the telephone, crisp and direct.
Each of your syllables
Carries in its heart the flaw of corruption.
Reap them. Burn the wild grasses.
Rare, spare the honey, tender it
In equal conscience. I said I would not.
Now I must admire the orange trees
Of Howard Baker's Terra Bella, Winters'
Palo Alto airedales at their distance,
And hear meanwhile the bells of Martin's wife
True to the sharp edge which will incise
Truth; it cannot all be cut away.

In the hills behind, old Indian fighters,
Suffragettes, the vote scarcely won
Readied to leave the vaulted blue-tiled well
Anytime for a New York jail.
They kept calling the journals all across the country
To wake up, get out a new edition
In pentameters if they couldn't manage a good *vers libre*.
And wake us still, dear Sara, Colonel, Caldwells,
Marie West, Taggard, Flanner into the chapparal
That will not slide the slopes but toughen
Into resolve to stick the firebreaks,
Sandy invasions and the hosts that blight the vines,
To draw the cup next year, new grapes.

Black to their coastal battlements
Sinclair Lewis wrote jokes for Jack London.
Somebody wasn't laughing. Jeffers bore
Human interest only at its darkest
The resources of flesh against its stone,
Of time against its heritage, of lamb
Against its higher bird.

To the city it's a very slow commute, South San Francisco
And Daly City, delaying quite a while
By sense of a tolerable alternative,
Then that irascible Rexroth's Potrero. Change.
Or as a spark at the flint, Laurence Hart's
Give me an image of rain, just one
Brilliant notation of the brilliantly spitty rain.
Translator MacIntyre bruises so easy

Early like Ginsberg late prescribing
Dog piss in gardens. In his garden
Hidden away, its mint and lettuce
Not susceptible.

Diamant too, Gleason, Duncan, Spicer, Schevill, Elliott,
Ammons, Stafford,
To the city and away to change.
Now the many poets
Are hard on each other. When they have gone away
They will write, say
This is a terrible land. Change
The focus of affection, move to remake
Interest, move to remake
Capital, that they not destroy, that they
Preserve, to change.

Sometimes they move back, now they come
On motor bikes, wife and child and manuscript
In the hip pocket. Here they are! The three-year-old
Child up to the rostrum to recite.
Stores and cafes, churches and grammar schools
Take up the poets of peace and gladness, of dices and black
        bones,
Aisles laid back with easy riding.
Unaccountable
Now so many
Each in his own center
To let the new terms be negotiable,
The makers measure change.

Center

How did you come
How did I come here
Now it is ours, how did it come to be
In so many presences?
Some I know swept from the sea, wind and sea,
Took up the right wave in their fins and seal suits,
Rode up over the town to this shore
Shining and sleek
To be caught by a tide
As of music, or color, or shape in the heart of the sea.
Was it you?

Was it you who came out from the sea-floor as lab into lab
Weightless, each breath
Bubbling to surface, swaying in currents of kelp plants,
Came in your cars
Freewayed in valleys millions of miles from the shore
To converge where the highways converge saying *welcome to
    here*,
And to where?
To tape and percussion, raga computers,
Rare texts and components of clay,
With the sea down away past the freeways and out of the
    town
To the blockbusting towers of learning and quiet
Shades of administering redwood,
Azure dome over all like a bellflower
And star above star.

Did you come
Out of borderlands dear to the south
Speaking a language Riveran, Nerudan, and saying

Aqui esta un hombre; my first lesson?
And come as Quixote, the man of romance
In its new century, tilting
At windmill giants of concrete,
Slim lance at the ready? Woe unto them
That join house to house, that lay field to field
Till there be no place that they may be alone
In the midst of the earth.

Did you come
With a handful of questions
Leaping like jewels
To shock answers, to start
Sparks of inquiry into the evening air?
I came as a kid
From that Midwest all recognize
As part of home,
To this another
Which the salt sea answered in its time
And Viscaíno mapped his ports upon.
You came
As concertmaster of the Philharmonic
As mayor of Del Mar
As reader of magnetic messages in DNA
As archivist for the time's poetry, or PTA,
As land-grant scholar
Holding his gray moon rocks.

What is this that we come to
Its walls and corridors
Gaping in space, its north lights
Seeking the north, its substance

Concrete brushed by the grain of its boards
Its boards reaching extension in all of their lengths
In architectural solidity?
It is
A break in the galaxies of our imagination. It needs our lives
To make it live.

A building, a dark hole in space,
Compact of matter,
Draws into it buzzing disinterests,
Ideologies.
Incomplete being
Enters into the dense room, emerges
Another, further,
Compact of matter, this is the place that we enter,
It paints pictures here and plays drums.
It turns us around and we emerge
Out of old space into the universe.
This building
Between buildings as between galaxies,
Between fields as between flights of fancy,
Will reshape our ears and turn us,
Our work of art
Beating in the breast like a heart.

What are we here for?
To err,
To fail and attempt as terribly as possible, to try
Stunts of such magnitude they will lead
To disasters of such magnitude they will lead
To learnings of such magnitude they will lend
Back in enterprise to substance and grace.

What learning allows for is the making of error
Without fatality.
The wandering off, the aberration,
Distortion and deviation
By which to find again the steady center,
And moving center.
What art allows for is the provisional
Enactments of such learning
In their forms
Of color and line, of mass and energy, of sound
And sense
Which bulk disaster large, create evil
To look it in its eye.
To forge
Villainies of the wars, to indispose
Villainies of petty establishment
To make them lead their lives in sound and sense
To no good end, that we may see them so.
To make mistakes
All of our own mistakes
Out of the huddle of possibilities
Into a color and form which will upbraid them
Beyond their being.

Give us to err
Grandly as possible in this complete
Complex of structure, risk a soul
Nobly in north light, in cello tone,
In action of drastic abandonment,
That we return to what we have abandoned
And make it whole.
Domesticate the brushed
Cement and wood marquee,

Fracture the corridors
Soften the lights of observation and renew
Structural kindness into its gentler shapes.

Out of the sea
The kelp tangles, out of the south
The cities crowd, out of the sky
The galaxies emerge in isolation
One from another, and the faces here
Look one to another in surprise,
At what has been made.
Look at the actual
Cliffs and canyons of this place,
People and programs, mass and energy
Of fact,
Look at the possible
Irradiating all these possibilities.

Praise then
The arts of law and science as of life
The arts of sound and substance as of faith
Which claim us here
To take, as a building, as a fiction takes us,
Into another frame of space
Where we can ponder, celebrate, and reshape
Not only what we are, where we are from,
But what in the risk and moment of our day
We may become.

Poetry from Illinois